The ParentNormal
CRASH Course

Everything Traditional Parenting Books Are Afraid to Tell You About Close Encounters of the Baby, Toddler and Third-Year Kind

By Chris Cate

Avamerolton Publishing

Copyright © 2016 Chris Cate

All rights reserved.

ISBN-13: 978-0692811061

For my kids Ava, Cameron and Colton who inspired this book and make every day worth the effort. And for my wife Lori who makes sure we survive this amazing time in our lives. I love you all.

There is no such thing as parenting advice.
There are only parenting warnings.

Consider yourself warned.

ParentNormal
[pair-uh-nt-nawr-muh-l]

Adjective.

1. relating to the supernatural new normal that begins upon first contact with a baby, toddler or threenager, involving a series of phenomena that require scientifically impossible amounts of love, generosity and devotion to survive.

Noun.

2. **the parentnormal**, parentnormal activity that is beyond explanation but is routine for parents.

Origin

ParentNormal activity dates back to the dawn of mankind and remains active today at dawn and often beforehand for all parents.

Example

Life is never the same once you've experienced the *ParentNormal*.

CRASH COURSES

The ParentNormal 101:   1

101 Things Every Parent Needs to Know Before Having a Baby

The ParentNormal 102:   37

102 Things Every Parent Needs to Know Before Their Baby Becomes a Toddler

The ParentNormal 103:   73

103 Things Every Parent Needs to Know Before Their Toddler Becomes a Threenager

Prepare to crash.

The ParentNormal 101

101 Things Every Parent Needs to Know Before Having a Baby

1

Some people believe you can become a great parent by watching other parents. But that's like believing you can become a great alligator wrestler by watching Animal Planet.

2

Raising a baby isn't like raising a dog. It's like being a dog. You're always sniffing butts.

3

Once you have a baby, the contact list in your phone will become the list of people you don't have time to contact.

4

Get used to wearing the same thing every day: spit up on your shirt.

5

Changing a diaper that doesn't need to be changed is an example of parenting being as good as it gets and as bad as it gets.

6

Building a tolerance to hearing a baby cry is like building a tolerance to coffee. At first it's awful, but then it becomes how you start your day.

7

Babies can act exactly the same whether they are clean or have poop in their diaper if you're wondering why you should be afraid, very afraid.

8

Baby hands are so small and gentle and clumsy and cute and armed with razorblades for fingernails. So approach with caution.

9

People without babies have mornings, afternoons and nights. People with babies only know bedtimes, past bedtimes and in need of naps.

10

If you've ever said something easy is like taking candy from a baby, you've never tried to take candy from a baby. A baby will cut you.

11

Forget taking a yoga class. Once you've taken 30 minutes to exit a baby's room in slow motion, you'll know every position well enough to teach a yoga class.

12

Babies are like whoopee cushions. As soon as you sit down, they make an unpleasant noise.

__13__

Baby clothes come in three sizes:
    a.) too small
    b.) fits for a day
    c.) can grow into it

__14__

Your baby's favorite food topping will be whatever is on top of your plate.

__15__

Don't bother saying, "You're going to wake the baby." Before you finish the words, your baby will already be awake.

__16__

Babies are like little sharks. They try to eat everything, you don't want to make them mad and they can't go backward.

__17__

Babies are the Michael Jordan* of the peek-a-boo game.

Michael Jordan the baseball player

__18__

When you get teary-eyed as a parent, you could be thinking about the good times or the hard times, but most likely it's the smell.

<u>19</u>

Never wear corduroy pants and try to put a baby to bed. You might as well be carrying a boombox playing *Wake Me Up Before You Go-Go*.

<u>20</u>

Babies don't ask to be picked up. They hold on tight to your leg until you do it.

<u>21</u>

You won't know what a baby's real bedtime is until they fall asleep, wake up and fall asleep again for the second, third and fourth time.

22

If you've never done an army crawl inside your house, you've probably never put a cranky baby to sleep and escaped the room successfully. Start practicing.

23

Wherever you are, wherever you go, remember, your baby is plotting to grab the sunglasses off your face to make it clear there is never a time when parents are cooler than their kids.

24

Babies aren't like us. They have us to put their pants on both feet at a time.

25

When your baby smiles at you for the first time, it's your baby's special way of letting you know they just pooped.

26

If you put shoes on a baby with 30 seconds to spare before leaving your home, you're going to have to do it again at least twice more.

27

It's okay to judge a book by its cover when the cover is missing. You can safely say that book has been in the hands of a baby.

28

Your new definition of 'scenic route' is going to be whatever road you're on when you see a sleeping baby in your rearview mirror.

29

Baby socks that look like shoes are the tuxedo shirts of baby clothing.

30

After you've changed a thousand diapers, it's the head-butts that stink the worst. Consider wearing boxing headgear to prevent concussions.

31

People will tell you their dog won't bite, but that's only because they haven't seen how hard a baby can pull a tail.

32

You will probably cry when your baby gets bigger and outgrows their baby clothes, but you will definitely cry when your baby grows too fast to wear so many of the expensive outfits you bought them.

33

Parents don't judge food quality based on taste, only the speed at which they can eat it.

34

Snap buttons on baby pajamas will make you realize what it's like to have the dexterity of a newborn baby.

35

March Madness for a new parent is when you don't know whether to dress your baby in a winter coat or shorts and you're always wrong.

36

When in doubt, give babies bubbles and get out of their way.

37

Babies love eating. The trick is denying them things they shouldn't eat like their feet, books and your phone.

38

Naptime is just the eye of the hurricane.

39

When restaurants give babies crayons, it's not for entertainment. It's to give them something to throw instead of the silverware. So be vigilant in restaurants that don't have crayons.

40

Bronzing your baby's shoes is a bad idea if you ever want your baby to learn to walk in them.

41

TVs might be getting smart, but not smart enough to tell you where your baby will hide the remote control.

42

According to babies, the difference between being held by someone sitting down and someone standing up is that if you're sitting down it doesn't count at all.

43

It's such a loving gesture when your baby leans in close, smiles and head-butts you in the nose. You don't soon forget it. Quite emotional.

44

If your schedule starts to fill up with very important meetings, your baby is about to get sick.

45

Strangers will know you're a new parent when you say "beep beep" to other adults instead of "excuse me" to exit an elevator.

46

Cutting a baby's fingernails is like cutting the red, yellow and green wires on a bomb, hoping each clip doesn't set off an explosion.

47

It's not baby food if you're a hungry adult. And you will be a hungry adult.

48

If you don't cry at the end of movies now, you will once you have a baby because that's when your baby will always wake up and prevent you from finishing movies.

__49__

The most comforting thing you can tell your baby isn't "I love you" or "You're going to be okay." It's "Are you ready to eat?"

__50__

When your baby learns to talk, you will realize all of those philosophical things you thought your baby was saying were just demands for more food.

__51__

The slowest you will ever drive is on the way home from the delivery room, because your baby only gets louder.

52

Don't bother getting jealous of your baby's soft skin. Their skin usually has baby food all over it.

53

Everything your baby drinks will look like it has pulp in it after they've taken a sip.

54

The f-bomb in your house is about to change to "fever."

__55__

If a baby was your life coach, they would tell you to find the one thing you love… and drop it.

__56__

The meaning of an all-nighter is very different for new parents, but the hangover still feels the same.

__57__

The only way a baby without a nap can be more tired is if they wake up five minutes early from a nap.

58

Childproof outlet plugs aren't just a great tool to keep your baby safe. They're also a great tool to rip your own fingernails off if you ever need a distraction from the late-night crying.

59

When a baby poops while you're changing a diaper, it's known as a dishonorable discharge. And these charges are made more often than a shopping addict charges credit cards at an outlet mall.

60

A baby's version of the fist bump is a head bump. So cute it hurts.

61

Children's books are much more entertaining if you read all of the rhymes like the characters are in a rap battle.

62

Living in a house with a baby is like living in a cage with a lion. You can't sleep, you have to tiptoe everywhere and heaven forbid you upset them.

63

Getting a baby to drink their medicine is like getting someone with arachnophobia to drink a spider, except harder.

64

When a baby lays their head on your shoulder, it's so sweet. It's like they are saying they love to use your shirt as a napkin.

65

Parents use baby monitors. Babies use squeaky floors. Nobody has alone time.

66

Board books are the #1 choice for babies who don't want to damage their books when they hit you in the face with them.

__67__

If you've never taken a baby toy out of a wrapper, just imagine unwrapping a DVD that has been triple-wrapped and tied up for no reason.

__68__

When your baby is teething, make sure to get plenty of teething toys. They will help relieve stress. You should probably get your baby some too.

__69__

Balancing life as a parent is like balancing a 50-foot stack of blocks on a pile of dirty clothes while your baby tries to knock them down.

__70__

What happens in Vegas is nothing compared to the gamble you make when you leave the house with a baby who hasn't taken a nap.

__71__

Babies are the opposite of Slinkies. Babies can only crawl upstairs and you beg them to stop.

__72__

With pinpoint accuracy, babies can throw something they desperately want exactly one centimeter out of your reach when you're driving.

73

The volume of a baby's cry has a direct correlation to the speed of their parent's car. Louder = faster.

74

Watching a baby sleep is like watching a beautiful sunset. Both are fleeting.

75

Babies don't have breakfast, lunch and dinner times. They have food spilling, stealing and throwing times. And those are all of the time.

__76__

If any good can come from stepping on sharp baby toys every day, it'll be the look on everyone's face when you're able to walk on hot coals without flinching.

__77__

The packaging says baby gate, but everybody knows it's really a climbing wall for babies and a hurdle for adults.

__78__

Babies have moments when they act older than their age. For instance, babies shake hands, eat prunes and go bald.

79

Baby on Board stickers are more impressive than 26.2 stickers because you can't put a number on the marathon it takes to raise a baby.

80

But there's no need for a Baby on Board sign. The swerving, volume of crying and spit-up on your windows will say it all.

81

The most likely time for a doorbell to ring, glass to crash, dog to bark, etc., is one second before a baby falls asleep.

82

Searching for a pacifier at night isn't like looking for a needle in a haystack. It's like looking for a straw of hay in a stack of needles. Physically and emotionally painful.

83

Babies are born with the ability to eat and sleep at the same time, which is far more impressive than tapping your head and rubbing your stomach. Don't underestimate them.

84

If babies could say whatever they wanted, they would tell whoever is in their face that their breath is awful.

<u>85</u>

A baby's sneeze is so cute that when your baby sneezes in your mouth you won't get upset. Disgusted, sure, but not upset.

<u>86</u>

Calling babies chubby is acceptable and a compliment. But don't follow that observation by saying your baby looks just like your spouse.

<u>87</u>

Clean Baby and Eating Baby are like Clark Kent and Superman. You never see them at the same time.

88

Your baby will try to get you to play catch... with your TV remote control when you're not looking.

89

The most unhelpful feature of pacifiers is that they disappear whenever they land on the floor.

90

A parent who says they've never thought their baby might be a genius is a liar.

91

For parents, it's always 5:00 somewhere else.

92

When your baby shakes your finger, they are probably taking the 'pull my finger' joke too far. Get the wipes.

93

Taking your baby out to dinner is a great idea until you take your baby out to dinner. Then it's like deciding to go on a diet right before going to an all-you-can-eat restaurant. Very bad decision.

94

Don't throw the baby out with the bathwater. In fact, don't throw babies or bathwater out. Your baby will throw out all of the bathwater for you.

95

Baby weight is like weather and wind chill. A baby that weighs 15 pounds can feel like 75 pounds.

96

When you wake up on a Saturday in a cold sweat thinking it's a workday, you'll always be right when you're a parent.

97

When your baby laughs, your heart will melt. Get yourself a bib.

98

Baby's gain head control faster than you think. As soon as you turn your head away from your baby, they will cry. Eventually you'll stop turning your head away. At that point, your baby will have total control over you.

99

The best photo album you can buy is a laptop. Too bad your actual lap top will always be occupied by a baby.

100

When new parents say they've got their hands full, it's not just a figure of speech. They have babies, wipes, bottles, toys, diapers, cameras, snacks, etc., in their hands.

101

Romantics wear their hearts on their sleeves. New parents wear spit up on their sleeves.

CHRIS CATE

The ParentNormal 102

102 Things Every Parent Needs to Know Before Their Baby Becomes a Toddler

1

You'll know you have a toddler when you're reading this book and someone tries to tell you something unimportant one inch from your face…and never stops telling you.

2

If there is something on the floor that can crumble into a million pieces, a toddler will step on it one second before you can get to it.

3

You say potato. I say potato. A toddler says, "No!" and throws it on the floor.

4

If toddlers spelled "momma" the way they sound it out, they would spell it Mommamommamommamommammommamommamoamommamomma!

5

Cleaning up after a toddler is like making your bed. As soon as you wake up, you have to do it again.

6

A romantic date for parents of toddlers is making it through half of a movie without having to wipe a butt or put a toddler back to bed.

7

Toddler paintings are like constellations. Somebody has to tell you what you're looking at, and then you see it, kind of.

8

All day long you will be reminding your toddler to use their words and all night long you will be reminding your toddler to stop using their words.

9

Toddlers never know for sure whether they want a healthy snack until the package is opened. And then they're certain they don't.

10

Sharing food with a toddler is like sharing an armrest with a stranger. Give them a little and they'll take it all.

11

There's a big difference between a toddler accidentally pooping in their pants and knowingly pooping in their pants, but the cleanup in the bathtub is the same crappy job.

12

95% of helping a toddler who falls down is trying not to laugh at how they fell down.

13

Toddlers sometimes think they need deodorant. But that always changes when they realize how bad it tastes.

14

A toddler's technique for telling secrets is leaning in close and wiping their nose on you.

15

Raising a toddler means lowering your standards for how much pee in a bed requires the sheets to be washed.

16

Toddlers walk around with a bag of snacks like most people do their phones: happy, captivated and very protective.

17

A parent's gravitational pull is extremely strong to toddlers, which is why they'll never leave our sides and how they're able to walk all over us.

18

Toddlers are the world's worst hiders and best mommy/daddy go-seekers.

19

When your toddler can't sleep, try counting sheep. It will help pass the time until it's time to get up.

20

When a toddler misses a nap, it's like buying a lottery ticket. You may get lucky and get to go to bed early, but odds are it just costs you.

21

Toddlers never have awkward silences, only nefarious silences.

22

Toddlers don't go out to eat with their families. They go out to eat with everybody in the restaurant.

23

Once you teach your toddler to cover their mouth when they cough, you will just need to get them to stop using your face as the cover.

24

Who needs a basketball goal when we've got a toilet?
- Toddlers Holding Important Things

25

Every toddler's internal alarm clock is set to shuffle from midnight to 6:00 a.m.

26

The ultimate wrap battle is a toddler versus a gift-wrapped present.

27

A toddler's idea of building blocks is throwing blocks until a pile eventually begins to form.

28

You will know when your toddler spills something because your toddler will slip and fall in it too.

29

When you catch a toddler red-handed, it's usually ketchup.

30

When a toddler has a crumby day, it's been a great day for them.

31

People who say don't sweat the small stuff have never tried to pick up a thousand goldfish crumbs from between the couch cushions.

32

A Toddler's Complete Bucket List:
1. Dump it out.

33

Everyone thinks toddlers in pajamas are cute – at least that's what you can tell yourself when your toddler has a meltdown during a wedding you arrive at 20 minutes late because you don't have time to keep fighting with your toddler about getting dressed.

34

Toddlers always want to dress up like cartoon characters: shirt and no pants.

35

Toddlers speak as clearly as the pictures they color on white paper with their white crayon.

36

You will agree to more requests from your toddler that you don't understand than requests you do understand, and you will do it enthusiastically for some reason.

37

Your new workout clothes are going to be whatever clothes you're wearing when your toddler is awake.

38

When a toddler says they want to talk on the phone, they really just want to hang up on somebody.

39

Toddlers are surprisingly bad at understanding their parents considering how often they walk around in their parents' shoes.

__40__

"You have the right to remain silent" is a line your toddler will interrupt with yelling before you can finish saying it.

__41__

Having a toddler leads to an increase in petting strangers' dogs from rarely ever to always.

__42__

If you don't know what hyperbole is you're doomed because parenting a toddler is the best and worst thing ever.

43

A toddler's favorite game to play at the pool is 'try to drown mommy and daddy.'

44

You will always know if your toddler was playing in a sandbox because the sandbox will fall out of their shoes as soon as they take them off.

45

Booster seats are excellent for helping toddlers who aren't quite tall enough to crawl onto the kitchen table.

46

A bedtime routine for a toddler mostly consists of parents saying "close your eyes" without success until sunrise.

47

A consequence of having a toddler is always having rotten bananas too. There is no way to buy the right amount for a toddler.

48

Toddlers are great at whispering if whispering means talking as quietly as they shout.

__49__

You will legitimately want to know if it is called a high chair because of its height or because your toddler acts like they're on drugs in a restaurant.

__50__

A hair in your food doesn't seem so gross once you have a toddler because there's usually been something much, much worse in your food, like a toddler hand.

__51__

Toddlers can hear the opening of a pantry or refrigerator from 250 miles away.

52

One day you will remember not to ask your kids what they want to drink because you will know it's whatever you're drinking.

53

Never throw away empty toilet paper rolls. That's wasting completely good telescopes.
- Toddlers

54

Toddlers dance the same way they cry: without inhibition.

__55__

Walking? No. Talking? No. The toddler milestone you will enjoy the most is when your toddler learns how to blow their nose before trying to kiss you.

__56__

Toddlers always go the extra mile... when they are running away from you in a public place.

__57__

The bright side of negotiating with your toddler about how many books to read at bedtime is that your toddler will quickly learn how to count to more than 100.

58

Dealing with a toddler who misses a nap is like dealing with a bear that misses their hibernation, except scarier.

59

Toddlers do adhere to the five-second rule. It's just that they believe five seconds is a VERY long time.

60

Want a great big hug from a toddler? Carry them into a swimming pool without their 'floaties' on. Enjoy the strong embrace.

61

When a toddler flips a toddler-size table, you won't know if it's because they're really angry or really happy.

62

A toddler's arch nemesis is a closed door.

63

A staycation for parents of toddlers is when a toddler stays in one place long enough for their parents to finish a drink.

64

It's always a great feeling when your schedule is cleared, except when it's your toddler clearing your sleep schedule. And you can consider it cleared already.

65

Covering your head with a pillow is the international sign of approval for toddlers to jump on your head.

66

Toddlers are very territorial. They mark their territory in their bed almost every night. Your bed is next.

67

In a toddler's house, sound asleep just means asleep until there is a sound of any kind.

68

Some nights you just have to read a book the way your toddler wants: from end to beginning.

69

Toddlers react to the sound of a parent tiptoeing out of a bedroom like parents react to the sound of a toddler shattering a glass of wine. Panic!

__70__

Every tower of blocks built with a toddler is the Tower of Babel. Nobody understands what's being said and the towers always collapse before completion.

__71__

Toddlers don't realize stuffed animals can't talk because they don't stop talking long enough for their stuffed animals to respond.

__72__

Toddlers don't see trashcans. They see lost and founds.

73

More toddlers should throw out the first pitch at baseball games because they always hit their target: an unsuspecting person's groin. Hilarious, except when it's you. (But expect it to be you.)

74

Every staircase is an escalator for toddlers who make you carry them.

75

If food companies calculated serving sizes for toddlers, they would need to multiply the adult serving size for snacks by 600% and subtract the serving size of healthy foods by 98%.

76

Watching a toddler learn to open doors is like watching the raptors in Jurassic Park learn to open doors.

77

When a toddler butt-dials someone, it's never an accident. It's tried hundreds of times before working.

78

After having kids, the closest you will feel to being in college again is when you make a midnight run to Walmart. The difference is it will be a trip for diapers.

79

On a stressful day, put sunglasses on your toddler and tell them it's getting dark, almost time for bed! It sounds crazy, but eventually you'll try anything. At least in this case they'll look adorable.

80

Toddlers use the floor like it's a condiment. Watch your step.

81

Trying to figure out the right plate and food combination for a toddler is like trying to complete a Rubik's Cube for the first time, every time.

82

Apples and oranges are exactly the same when it comes to how far your toddler can and will throw slices.

83

Toddlers aren't following you. They're waiting in line to be in charge after you. So be nice.

84

Toddler shoes don't come in pairs. They're only found one-at-a-time in remote areas of the world.

85

How will you know when your toddler is ready for their first haircut? You'll find gum in their hair.

86

There's a brief window of time when a winter coat perfectly fits a toddler, and it always begins the day the zipper breaks.

87

Every room is a changing room to a toddler.

88

A toddler's missing shoe won't appear until you're already late.

89

Most people use filler words such as "um" or "uh" to fill gaps in speech. Toddlers fill their gaps in speech (and everybody else's gaps in speech) with "hold me!"

90

Every time a bell rings, an angel gets their wings. Every time a toddler cries, a parent hears ringing in their ears.

<u>91</u>

A toddler's definition of Band-Aids: Adhesive bandages for some injuries but mostly the imagined ones.

<u>92</u>

Sharing is a foreign concept to toddlers until you have something they want. Then, they're experts on the subject.

<u>93</u>

A toddler's first step is all over you. And it gets worse when they learn how to walk.

94

A power nap for a toddler is when they make you stay in their room until they fall asleep. Total power move.

95

Transitioning toddlers from a crib to a bed is like transitioning them from a car seat to a surfboard in a hurricane.

96

'No more tears' shampoo? You will be lucky if you can get 'no more tears' bathwater for a toddler.

__97__

Even worse than the terrible twos are the terrible "me toos!"

__98__

After a while, you'll stop giving your toddler so many gifts and start giving your toddler so many bribes.

__99__

Toddlers love riding bikes. They just don't enjoy pedaling. Prepare to push uphill, pull downhill and never find level ground.

100

Feeding a toddler mostly consists of lying about how good a food tastes.

101

Parents of toddlers are always going in the same direction: to get another paper towel.

102

The sound of a toddler snoring in your ear every night will be your blessing and your curse.

CHRIS CATE

The ParentNormal 103

103 Things Every Parent Needs to Know Before Their Toddler Becomes a Threenager

1

Parenting threenagers is like hosting Jeopardy. Threenagers are always asking questions about the things you've already answered for them.

2

No two words slow down a threenager more than the phrase "hurry up."

3

The only thing threenagers can't lose is their voice.

4

If you want to completely confuse a parent, tell them their threenager was so well behaved.

5

Minivans don't come with cup holders. They just come with shallow, circular trashcans for threenagers to fill with sticky things.

6

Artwork by threenagers is like mail. It covers your tables, keeps accumulating and it's hard to tell what to throw away.

7

You can run a mile backwards with flip-flops on faster than a threenager can walk ten feet with the television on.

8

When threenagers say please, it's usually because they're tired of yelling so much for something.

9

You will wish hindsight wasn't 20/20 when your threenager asks you to wipe them.

10

The only thing threenagers hate more than getting in a bath is getting out of a bath.

11

It's impossible to pick up after threenagers. Seriously. You can't pick up after people who never pick up anything the first time.

12

If there's ever a moment of silence in your car, you are destined to blow it by pointing at something your threenager will somehow not see.

13

Watching a threenager for two hours is like watching a theatre production of *Die Hard*.

14

Threenagers talk like everything they say is a "reply all" message to everybody in the room with them.

15

Fish are a good first pet, but they still have challenges. The challenges aren't life and death – just death, indescribable-to-a-threenager death.

16

You will need a five-year plan to figure out what to do during the time it takes your threenager to go to the bathroom.

17

Threenagers are more afraid of getting shampoo in their eyes than anything you warn them about that can actually poke out an eye.

18

When your threenager is crying loudly in their room, be concerned. When your threenager is being quiet in their room, be VERY concerned.

19

All threenagers need glasses. If you only give them one glass they'll break it and need another one.

20

When your threenager assures you they will clean up their mess, you will know what your dentist must feel like when you assure them you will floss.

21

Threenagers have an 85% chance of putting their shoes on the wrong feet.

22

If you think texting and driving is dangerous, you don't want to know how dangerous it is to be parenting a threenager and driving.

23

The best judge of a threenager's week at daycare is how many days they come home wearing a different shirt.

24

You can search the entire internet faster than a threenager can search their room for a pair of shoes in the middle of their room.

25

The only knock-knock joke a threenager knows is the one that has a million knocks and no punch line.

26

Parents don't go on vacation. Kids go on vacation while their parents babysit them.

27

Threenagers can't give you the silent treatment. They can only leave you speechless.

28

You will always know when you're the farthest distance from a bathroom because that's always when your threenager says they have to go potty, NOW!

29

The snooze button for threenagers is ice cream. But when the alarm sounds, get ready for a brain freeze.

30

The 80/20 Rule of Parenting Threenagers: You must tell a threenager a rule 80 times for them to hear it 20 times so they finally follow it for the first time.

31

The line between disciplining a threenager and Mommy and Daddy getting a much-needed break for a few minutes is very blurred during "timeouts."

32

A threenager's favorite show is the show they absolutely don't want to watch ever again in two minutes.

33

As the parent of a threenager, you want to open doors for them. As someone who pays air-conditioning bills, you must close every door they open, which is all of them.

34

If you need help getting your threenager to come when you call, just ask if there's anyone who can help blow out a candle.

35

If a threenager ever asks to sleep in one morning, don't get too excited. There's a 100% chance that just means they want to sleep in your bed.

36

It's so special when a threenager falls asleep on your shoulder because it means they must've been awake for at least 36 hours for that to happen.

37

Threenagers may dance like nobody's watching, but they also pick their nose like nobody's watching. So let's call it a draw.

38

Threenagers love surprise birthday parties. They will surprise you with the news it's their birthday several times a year.

39

When something is truly innovative, threenagers refer to it as 'the greatest thing since sliced bread without crust.'

40

When a threenager brings you a drink, it's not necessary to tip. They've already taken a 20% sip.

41

The best emergency contact for a threenager is the pizza delivery guy.

42

If you want to tell a threenager a scary story, tell them about the time they went to bed early. If they scream, you can explain it's not a true story. It's pure fantasy.

43

Parenting threenagers has a two drink minimum, because threenagers are never happy with the first drink you give them.

44

Teeth grinding is the go-to option for threenagers who are too tired to stay awake while they're keeping you awake.

45

A good trip to the grocery store with a threenager is making it to the checkout line with more things to buy than things the threenager ate, broke or contaminated.

46

A threenager's favorite pediatrician is a Band-Aid, whether there's blood involved or not.

47

90% of a threenager's teeth-brushing process involves falling off a stool.

48

A threenager's ideal night light is something bright enough to light Yankee Stadium that also requires a parent to remain close by.

<u>49</u>

Threenagers are as irrationally afraid of the dark as parents are irrationally afraid of jumping into a cold swimming pool.

<u>50</u>

If you want to leave somewhere on time, it's a good idea to start telling your threenager it's time to go before you even get there.

<u>51</u>

You can't win a staring contest with a threenager. They don't blink when you tell them it's naptime.

52

An easy way to turn a threenager's clothes into Easter clothes is to give a threenager sidewalk chalk. Within seconds, their clothes will change into Easter colors.

53

A threenager's preferred method to fix something is to reboot, which in layman's terms means to kick it again.

54

Threenagers think pennies are worth millions of dollars, which is why they're the best people to give cash birthday presents.

55

Threenagers can't understand why they are so hard to put to sleep because they put their stuffed animals to sleep so easily.

56

The only thing threenagers know about a curfew is that's the sound they make when they sneeze on you.

57

You probably shouldn't yell fire in a crowded theater, but you definitely shouldn't yell SPIDER! in a crowd of threenagers.

58

If a threenager has two options or a surprise third option, they'll always choose the surprise, then change their mind until they get all options.

59

When a threenager has a theory, it always involves a big bang.

60

When you hear footsteps at night, it will probably be a burglar…a short, clumsy, unapologetic, three-year-old burglar stealing any chance you had of a good night's sleep.

__61__

Threenagers aren't impressed by adult supervision – not unless it's the super-vision that allows you to see through walls and stuff.

__62__

You know you have threenagers when somebody at work asks you about the stickers on your hands and you don't consider taking them off.

__63__

When parents of threenagers are invited to a party that starts at nine o'clock, it's always nine o'clock in the morning.

__64__

Time flies when you're having… your threenagers spend the day at their grandparent's house.

__65__

When an adult screams without reason, they are probably crazy. Stay away. When a threenager screams without reason, they are probably just singing. Compliment them.

__66__

There's always a day when kids realize their parents aren't superheroes. For most kids, it's when they're three-years-old and they ask their parents to draw a horse for them.

__67__

There are no stay at home moms/dads, only work at home moms/dads whose work is even harder when they have to take their kids outside the home.

__68__

Threenagers are so popular…with ants.

__69__

When you see a threenager playing to your left and then see that threenager playing to your right, it's hard to know whether they are getting faster or you're just falling in and out of sleep from exhaustion. The answer is both.

70

If your phone isn't working, there's a good chance your threenager put your phone in airplane mode. In other words, there's a good chance your threenager threw it.

71

You don't think you play favorites with your kids until you realize you put your threenager in the backseat of the minivan every time.

72

When a threenager asks you to close your eyes and follow them, the surprise is always them walking you into the corner of a table.

73

A threenager's sick bucket is always one second too far away.

74

Threenagers aren't afraid to say what they think. Too bad they're terrified to think about something other than what we're most insecure about.

75

The reason Hollywood hasn't made a movie about the life of a threenager is because every stuntman and stuntwoman is too scared to attempt even the most mundane acts of a threenager.

76

Every day is summer with a threenager because every day is longer with a threenager.

77

A threenager can meltdown faster than ice cream in a microwave but nobody will know why or how a threenager does weird things like put ice cream in a microwave.

78

When life gives you threenagers, don't make lemonade. The sugar rush will make them rush into bad decisions at an even faster pace than usual.

<u>79</u>

Threenagers love going down slides, mostly because it means they get to walk back up them.

<u>80</u>

A threenager playing piano will make you want to headbang, as in bang your head against a wall.

<u>81</u>

You might think it's wise to emulate the early bird that gets the worm, but that will change when your threenager wakes up early every day and accomplishes nothing more than catching a few dead worms.

82

The windows lock button in cars isn't to prevent kids from falling out. It's to prevent threenagers from rolling windows up and down in perpetuity with their feet.

83

The reason threenagers want to use the most inconvenient and dirty bathrooms is so they have more options to gross you out.

84

A jar with a stick and a blade of grass inside is the most deadly weapon a threenager can carry. Animals beware.

<u>85</u>

A threenager always gives 110%... of their vegetables to the trashcan, which includes the extra 10% of your vegetables that you didn't want and tried to give them.

<u>86</u>

Threenagers think magic is real, so there's no point trying to explain their lost toys can't just disappear when they make that claim.

<u>87</u>

When you think your threenager is making up their own gibberish language, remember that's what your grandmother thought when she first heard slang too.

88

It's important to build trust with your threenager, so when you're in a hurry they will believe you when you tell them that their socks don't need to match.

89

Love your threenager enough to always let them help you cook and be smart enough to never eat what they cook.

90

Plot Twist: Threenagers are the monsters scaring everybody at night.

91

The password for a threenager's blanket fort these days requires an uppercase letter, lowercase letter and a number.

92

You will be most jealous of your threenager when you realize they don't know what day it is and they don't even care.

93

Threenagers overthink what foods they love and hate so much that they've foolishly tricked themselves into thinking hot dogs are a delicacy. Use this information to your advantage.

94

If you don't like snoring now, you will once you have a threenager. You will wait all day to hear them make that sound.

95

Threenagers must think they can brush their teeth with the bathroom sink because that's where they drop all the toothpaste before they brush.

96

Some people say the last puzzle piece is the easiest, but those people must not have threenagers. The last puzzle piece for anyone with a threenager is the hardest because the threenager has always lost it.

97

Winning a game against a threenager is so much worse than losing.

98

If you want to save some money, change your vacation plans from going to Disney World to going to your own mailbox. A threenager will love that trip more than all of the rides at Disney World combined.

99

A great thing about threenagers today is they already know how to recycle. For instance, they say the same thing again and again and again and again and again…

100

Threenagers get more peanut butter and jelly sandwiches on their face than they get in their stomach, and that's exactly how they like it.

101

Threenagers act like it's their mission to beat natural selection.

102

Threenagers can stare at the refrigerator for hours and hours and never pick out something to eat, but they can complete their birthday and Christmas lists for a full decade in the span of a 30-second toy commercial.

__103__

The first three years of parenthood are one long game of charades. The following years are just bonus rounds in which your kids can talk well enough to give you riddles as clues.

THE PARENTNORMAL CRASH COURSE

CHRIS CATE

ACKNOWLEDGMENTS

A million thanks to my wife, Lori, for being my best friend and an incredible momma to our three kids. I love you.

Thanks to Ava, Cameron and Colton for being my daily inspiration. I am so proud to be your daddy. I love you more every day.

And thanks to my parents, Keith and Paula, for your generosity, patience, encouragement and love. You continue to show me how to be a great parent.

ABOUT THE AUTHOR

Chris Cate is a three-time parent, all-time minivan driver and no-time sleeper. He also hosts the ParentNormal Comedy Podcast, which can be heard on iTunes and at www.parentnormal.com.

Cate is a contributor to the Huffington Post, McSweeney's Internet Tendency, Scary Mommy and many other parenting sites. He has also been featured on the Huffington Post's weekly list of funniest parents on Twitter more than 75 times and been recognized for his parenting humor on BuzzFeed, The A.V. Club, Scary Mommy, TODAY Parents and more parenting sites.

Follow Chris Cate on Twitter @ParentNormal, Instagram @ParentNormal and on Facebook at www.Facebook.com/TheParentNormal.

CHRIS CATE

ParentNormal.com

CHRIS CATE

Bonus Tip:
Tell your baby, toddler or threenager that this is the most important page in the book so when they eventually rip out a page, get artistic with makeup or spill yogurt, it will be this page that gets damaged the most.

CHRIS CATE

Made in the USA
Lexington, KY
10 January 2017